A STUDY FOR THE DEPARTMENT OF HEALTH

INCLUSIVE PLAY

Supporting provision for disabled children

Pat Petrie, Pamela Storey and Mano Candappa

Thomas Coram Reseach Unit
Institute of Education, University of London

First published in 2002 by the Institute of Education, University of London,
20 Bedford Way, London WC1H 0AL

100 years of excellence in education

© Institute of Education, University of London 2002

British Library Cataloguing in Publication Data:
A catalogue record for this publication is available from the British Library

ISBN 0 85473 666 2

Design by Tim McPhee
Page make-up by Cambridge Photosetting Services

Production services by
Book Production Consultants plc, Cambridge

Printed by Watkiss Studios Ltd, Biggleswade, Beds

Contents

5. Practice within inclusive play services

6. Conclusions

Acknowledgements

The authors wish to thank the Department of Health for funding the Inclusive Play project. We also acknowledge all who contributed to the understandings that inform this report: children and parents, play providers, personnel drawn from different local government departments and from voluntary sector organisations. We are grateful to them for giving their time and sharing their experience. We wish to thank Sandra Melville and Bernard Spiegal for conducting some of the interviews and we are grateful, too, for the support of administrative staff at the Thomas Coram Research Unit, especially that of Sharon Lawson, the project secretary.

Introduction

Service providers must not discriminate against disabled people (including children) by refusing to provide any service which is provided to members of the public, providing a lower standard of service or offering a service on less favourable terms. These requirements came into force on 2 December 1996.

Since 1 October 1999 services providers have had to take reasonable steps to:

- Change a policy, practice or procedure which make it impossible or unreasonably difficult for disabled people to make use of services;
- Provide an auxiliary aid or service if it would enable (or make it easier for) disabled people to make use of services; and
- Provide a reasonable alternative method of making services available to disabled people where a physical feature makes it impossible or unreasonably difficult for disabled people to make use of them.

From 2004 service providers will have to take reasonable steps to remove, alter or provide reasonable means of avoiding physical features that make it impossible or unreasonably difficult for disabled people to use a service.

Whilst the provision of education is excluded from these requirements, other services provided by early years providers, e.g. childcare, would be covered.

(DfEE, 2001: 15–16)

The Disability Discrimination Act and the Quality Protects programme form the policy background to this report. The report presents findings from a study conducted between April and September 2000 on inclusive out-of-school services for disabled children. It is based on the social model of disability: that is, it sees disability as socially constructed and a source of social exclusion (this is discussed at greater length in the report on a study conducted in parallel to the one reported here (Petrie *et al.*, forthcoming).

The focus of the work was on services where one or more of the children attending were perceived by service providers as disabled. That is, these were services where the providers had taken at least some special steps, over and above their usual procedures, in order to receive the children. This is far from a complete definition of what is required for a service to be truly inclusive, with all that term implies for the development of policy and practice. It was, however, a working definition for the purposes of the research. We were interested in examining the practice of providers who included disabled children among their users, in the knowledge that some of this wider group would operate in an *ad hoc* fashion, while others would consciously strive for integration and inclusivity. We concentrated on the service provider's viewpoint, because the perspectives of service users had been central to an earlier study (Petrie *et al.*, 2000) and here we wished to understand the structural underpinning of inclusive provision.

The report also draws on relevant material from earlier studies (Petrie, 1994; Petrie and Poland, 1996; Petrie and Poland, 1998; Petrie *et al.*, 2000), especially *Out-of-school Lives, Out-of-School Services* (Petrie *et al.*, 2000), which explored the out-of-school lives of disabled children, including their use of playschemes and after-school clubs.

As a group, disabled children are defined in the Children Act 1989 and its Guidance (Department of Health, 1991) as being 'in need'. Out-of-school services can deliver the family support that local authorities seek to provide for families in need, and are specifically mentioned in the Guidance to the Act. They meet the needs expressed by the parents of disabled children for what are sometimes called respite services, as well as more child-centred needs identified for example by Beresford (1995: 33–4). In earlier work, we found that families with a disabled child were especially pleased with the play opportunities offered by out-of-school services, by their function as respite care and because they reduced social isolation for both parents and children. However, fieldwork observations and information supplied by service providers suggested that, to the discomfort of staff and children alike, staff were often not properly trained or supported for work with disabled children.

> [W]e found that half of the six services we visited fell short of standards which would ensure the children's well being, safety and comfort. . . . In some ways, services for disabled children suffered similar problems as those to be found in the others described in this book: inadequate material resources, untrained staff, an underdeveloped pedagogy for working with any children including disabled children.
>
> (Petrie *et al.*, 2000: 88)

This earlier work raised important questions regarding the effectiveness of services in providing play and care for disabled children and identified some of the organisational factors that made for success or failure, ranging from daily practice with children, communication with parents, to staff training and funding issues. In out-of-school services, as in other services, the needs of disabled children, and the need to provide for disabled children still receive low priority. The Audit Commission recently reported that:

> Two aspects of children's services stand out as being the most underdeveloped and least responsive to need – services for children and young people with disabilities . . . and services for children with mental health problems. Of all the children who may use social care services, children with a disability are the most visible . . . and yet they remained poorly served. They frequently find it harder to gain access to services, wait longer for assessment, and receive poorer quality services – often from staff lacking specific knowledge and skills.
>
> (Audit Commission, 1999: 23)

The Department of Health's Quality Protects programme seeks to address the inequalities that disabled children and their families experience, by the provision of earmarked grants, and by an emphasis on the inclusion of disabled children in mainstream services. Government policy, expressed in a range of other measures, from the Children Act 1989 to The Disability Discrimination Act 1995, stresses that disabled people should have access to mainstream services. This mirrors the developing understanding that disability, with the disadvantage that accompanies it, is socially produced, and echoes the impetus for mainstream schooling as enshrined in education acts over the last twenty years. The most recent of these, the Special Educational Needs and Disability Act 2001, enhances the rights of children with special educational needs to be educated in mainstream schools, and places new duties on LEAs and schools to provide for disabled pupils as favourably as for non-disabled pupils.

The Inclusive Play study

The study that is reported here looked specifically at inclusive play, care and recreational services for disabled children (henceforth, 'out-of-school services'). Disabled children sometimes attend *special* out-of-school services provided, perhaps, in special schools or as part of play provision within a local authority. Special play services can have much to offer children and families, but their major drawback is that they separate children from their non-disabled peers. In so doing, they can compound the social exclusion experienced by children and families. Inclusive services, on the other hand, are attended by disabled and non-disabled children alike.[1]

The Inclusive Play study aimed to identify how local authorities, the voluntary sector and providers can support inclusive play and care services for disabled children. The intention was to offer a framework for improved practice in out-of-school services for disabled children so as to 'increase the number of disabled children who use inclusive play and leisure services, including playschemes, after-school clubs and pre-school provision, with appropriate support if necessary.[2]

More specifically the research set out to:

- examine the provision of inclusive services for disabled children;
- identify the characteristics of different models of integrated services and look at their practice;
- identify the organisational supports that underpin good practice in integrated service provision.

Good practice is here seen as activity that supports providers and staff in delivering a service which is inclusive in:

- its intake of disabled and non-disabled children;
- the integration of disabled children in daily activities;
- serving different ethnic groups within the local community;
- being socially and physically accessible for children with a range of physical and sensory disabilities, learning, behavioural and communication difficulties;
- offering the same level of service, in terms of days and hours, to disabled children as to others;
- providing the means by which disabled children and their parents/carers may access provision (e.g. the provision of information, adequate transport, support with fees).

The study involved interviews in fourteen local authorities with local authority and voluntary sector personnel, visits to 32 out-of-school services, and interviews with playworkers and with children. The design of the study and the sample are described in Appendix 1.

The report is set out in five chapters. It looks first at the value of inclusive play to parents, to children and to social services. The second chapter describes the two main types of inclusive provision, mainstream and reversed integration, and at some of their perceived limitations. Chapter three examines the infrastructures required for inclusive services, in terms of staffing and premises. The fourth chapter looks at the roles of the local authority and other agencies in supporting inclusive provision. A final chapter sets out what might be described as 'good practice' in the daily activities of inclusive services.

1. We should say that to attend an inclusive service rather than a special service was not a prime consideration for the majority of users interviewed for the earlier study: they rarely had a choice between services. However, with the continuing expansion in out-of-school services, under the government's 1997 National Childcare Strategy, the question of a place for disabled children within mainstream services comes to the fore.
2. Local Authority Circular LAD (98) 28: *Quality Protects Programme: Transforming children's services*. London: DoH: Sub-objective 6.3, Objectives for Children's Social Services.

1 The value of inclusive play services

Parents' views

The value of play services for disabled children was summed up in an earlier study thus:

> Many problems were seen to be alleviated by the child's attending after-school or holiday play services, however they were organised. These were problems which could have been alleviated by other forms of respite care – and some children received this, residentially or by day. Nevertheless, mothers were able to distinguish the benefits which children derived specifically from playschemes. They were pleased that to some extent their children could be 'ordinary' children at the playschemes, that there they had greater freedom, companionship with other children and varied activities, sometimes of educational benefit. They appreciated that the children were safe and that staff were communicative about the children. They liked it when staff were consistent with parents and the school in their methods of confronting challenging behaviour.
>
> (Petrie *et al.*, 2000: 171)

Quotations from mothers taking part in a group interview as part of this work illustrate this:

> The main reason I would send Nicholas to an after-school project is to make friends in the community.

> Well I personally think it's been absolutely wonderful. Because one of the problems with children with handicaps of whatever nature is their isolation, you know that they are very drawn to . . . even if they're not communicating with other children, but watching what other children do is giving them ideas.

> Katie learns lot at the playground. She learns to share, to take turns, to wait, but at school, they could not get her to do anything, they said she was not compliant.

> Education is about being able to make choices, about taking risks. We can't wrap them up in cotton wool.

> Play service can be early intervention.

> I would fold up if my child could not go to Playscheme.

Children's views

In both this and the earlier study, many disabled children were not able to express in words their own feelings about out-of-school services. From the point of view of the researcher, however, they appeared to enjoy many of the same things about play services as other children. They seemed to appreciate space in which to play where this was available, children to be with and the companionship of adults who could support their play and other activities (many examples appear in earlier work, see Petrie, 1994; Petrie *et al.*, 2000). On the other hand, they sometimes displayed signs of distress when they were restricted as to movement and activity – for example during long periods on a bus, or when indoor premises were over-crowded on rainy days. For some, their participation in a service seemed to be reduced to that of the mere spectators to others' activities, sometime willingly sometimes not (this is looked at in greater detail below (pp. 23–4).

In answer to the question 'What do you like?' children responded:

> The soft play room. – Playing with puzzles and games. – The PlayStation. – Playing in the ball pool. – Outings. – Swimming.

> The staff – they are kind, and do things with you.

> They're just here to make sure we're safe

> – and to entertain you.

An 11-year-old boy said about a playscheme he attended regularly:

> It's lots of fun for any one. For a child who is disabled or anything. It's very welcoming for everyone. They'll never put you down. If something is wrong they will help you. N. (play leader) is like my second mother. Much better than school. You can do every-thing here if you use your imagination. This place feeds and lives on imagination, if people had no imagination this place would die. You can do cool things, you go on trips, like to the park. You act plays, like the Wizard of Oz. The staff are cool, when you're bored, they try to cheer you up and keep you company. You can do whatever you want.

However, it is not only disabled children who may benefit from inclusive provision. One play co-ordinator saw the value of inclusive play from the viewpoint of the non-disabled child:

> I actually think that if children learn about inclusive play then they are going to learn as adults about inclusive life. I think children need to be encouraged to grow up in that environment so then it is not a problem for them when they are older. . . . So I think it is good if you can start here, educating the children – in fact they can educate us because they don't have a problem. We are the ones that give them the problem. I think able-bodied children learn a lot from children with disabilities.
>
> It's the core philosophy of the project that children benefit [from] playing with their peers, be they disabled or non-disabled. And it's beneficial on both sides of the relationship.

And a group of non-disabled children, aged 10–11 at a mainstream playscheme talked about what they perceived to be the value of inclusive play.

Boy: It's a good opportunity for them to get out and do things that they won't usually be able to do.

Girl 1: And nobody really minds them being here either, 'cos like you get to play with them as well.

Boy: And they make new friends, 'cos disabled people don't get as much chance to make friends as everyone else usually does.

Girl 2: Yeah

Boy: So they get the chance to come in, make a lot of friends.

The same children went on to discuss how children, some with severe physical disability, were able to join in with the activities:

Girl 1: They like going on the bouncy castle.

Girl 2: But they don't actually go inside.

Boy: A lot of them don't actually go in it because there's like a green pad along the front and . . .

Girl 1: They go on that, they lie on that.

Boy: And when everyone is bouncing, it goes up and down.

Girl 2: And the helpers are really good to them.

Girl 1: Yeah, the helpers are nice to everybody as well, not just to them. They like to talk to us as well.

Although the passage may seem 'benevolent', it can also be read as revealing a social distance between the non-disabled children and the others, representing a divisive 'us and them' perspective. This social gap is not always apparent in play services: playworkers comment that children do not seem to notice the difference between disabled and non-disabled children. However, local practice can stand in the way of integration. In the above case the children refer to the 'helpers', the key workers allocated to the disabled children. We discuss below how such workers can form a barrier around their charges and other ways in which integration can be achieved.

Value of inclusive play services to social services

Social service personnel indicated the following ways in which inclusive provision is valuable. First, services are available during holidays when family respite needs are greatest. A social service manager in the Midlands said that the school holidays, particularly the long summer break can be a 'traumatically demanding time for parents' and a time when local authority respite provision is under pressure. The alternative domiciliary respite care provided by a private agency is sometimes seen as less acceptable to the family and less reliable than a play service.

Also, play services can be a cheaper alternative to either domiciliary or residential services. A social services manager working in London said: 'We want to provide low-cost and high-volume services and not the other way round – we want to provide more services in the community rather than respite care at several hundred pounds per night.' In addition, the inclusivity of play provision can be appealing to local authority social services and play services and for some is an explicit objective as part of their policy to respect social diversity and to provide equal opportunities for disabled children.

2 Two forms of inclusive services

There are two main types of inclusive services: what is sometimes referred to as 'reversed integration', and mainstream provision. Each type has its champions and each its detractors.

Reversed integration

Services used substantially by disabled children, and planned around their needs are sometimes referred to as reversed integration services, in that non-disabled children are thereby integrated into settings intended primarily for disabled children. Sometimes these may be held in a purpose-built setting, such as a special school or a special adventure playground, planned for disabled children. They are fully equipped for disabled children, with special ramps, lifts, toilets, washing facilities, toys and play equipment. Typically, brothers and sisters of the disabled child and perhaps other children living in the immediate locality also attend, but non-disabled children are usually in the minority.

> I think as soon as you bring siblings in, it becomes a lot more accountable. I don't know, I feel that way, because my son is non-verbal, he's pretty good at using his communication book but also his nature is a bit passive . . . if they did leave him just sitting there for an hour, I don't really know if he would tell me about it but A. (his sister) would or some of the other kids would tell me, who were more able, you know, so I like the idea that it is an integrated thing.
>
> (Mother of disabled child)

The advantages of reversed integration, as put forward by staff and parents, are that services organised on this basis can cater adequately for the disabled child, so long as experienced staff are present. They are seen to be safe and appropriate settings. Since they provide also for non-disabled children, the disabled children are not socially isolated. Such services were also seen as flagships that raised awareness of disabled play and, in many cases, formed the basis for subsequent more widespread mainstream developments. Nevertheless, other informants believed that reversed integration was only a small improvement on segregated special services. One, who put this point of view strongly, said that they were ghettos for disabled children, with able-bodied children attending as mere tokens of inclusivity. A further disadvantage of reversed integration schemes is that, for the disabled children who attend them, they are rarely locally based since they are usually located in specialised schools or centres. Disabled children who attend these schemes are less likely to meet and integrate with other children living near them. The position of their siblings is also worth consideration: might it be better for siblings to see their brothers and sisters properly supported in a local mainstream service, rather than being brought together with other children who have a variety of impairments – thus emphasising, for them and others, the function of impairment as a basis for social organisation?

Mainstream inclusive play

The second form of inclusive practice was represented by services that admitted a small minority of disabled children to a mainstream after-school club or holiday playscheme. These services were not designed specifically for disabled children and, sometimes, special measures had to be taken to enable them to attend. For the most part, such measures necessitated extra staffing rather than at any modification of the premises (see pp. 12–13, 22).

Those who spoke in favour of admitting disabled children to mainstream provision did so on the grounds that such provision mirrored more closely the local community and the 'real world'; disabled and non-disabled children mixing together was seen as healthy for both groups. For some, good practice meant including all children in the general activities of the services. This could mean, for example, taking an 'autistic' child to the cinema, in spite of any potential difficulties, because to do so serves the aims of social integration. A further perceived advantage was that mainstream provision tends to be more locally based than the reversed integration model – which is likely to be a somewhat central service for a more widely spread population of children.

Some parents and staff expressed doubts about mainstream provision, including fears that the children's needs for safety were not adequately met, that the disabled child could 'get lost' in mainstream provision, that non-disabled children claimed too much staff time, and that the level of activity might be 'too much' for some disabled children.

One, probably unique, service included in the study was a mainstream adventure playground that had at one time housed a separate, specially equipped service for disabled children. Over time, the children themselves had initiated integration between the two groups. Children had got to know each other just because they were using the same premises and had begun, informally, to join in each other's activities. As these contacts developed, staff raised questions about the need for separation between the two groups. Eventually, the managing body made decisions that enabled the two groups to be brought together, so that all the children could benefit more fully from the many play opportunities on offer, from the large-scale adventure play equipment to the sensory room accessible previously only to the disabled children. The policy addressed the problem of the more able-bodied children monopolising attractive equipment to the detriment of disabled children, and used a risk assessment model (see p. 29) for looking at children's participation in adventurous play. However, while the playground operated on an 'open door' basis for non-disabled children, disabled children were rationed as to their attendance because of the concomitant need for increased staffing.

Some informants believed that the barriers to admitting disabled children into mainstream services were to be found more in the hearts and minds of providers and staff, than in any material constraints. They pointed out that buildings were usually accessible without modification and that, with good will, any initial difficulties could be overcome. They believed that staff were unsure about working with disabled children only because they had never done so, and had, knowingly, met few disabled people, face to face, in the course of their private or working lives. Such a view suggests that a disinclination to accept disabled children was both based on social discrimination against disabled people and continued and reinforced it. However, one experienced provider expressed her concerns that the whole issue of inclusion operates on what she described as a 'good natured scheme'. She said 'We wobble our way through', explaining that this meant being accommodating when requests were made and giving places to children with disabilities without always getting the additional staff or funding required. Consequently, the care given to the children was often less than the best and that because of 'corner cutting', the inclusive service offered was, overall, of a poorer quality than they would have liked.

Other providers talked of finding themselves under pressure to permit children with disabilities to 'jump the queue'. Whereas parents of other children accepted that they must wait for a vacancy and that provision was on a 'first come first served' basis, social workers and health visitors were sometimes reported to put pressure on service providers for children to 'jump the queue'. There was evidence, however, that providers were not always willing to succumb to such pressure and might refuse to take children with disabilities, sometimes using procedural criteria as a rationale.

> The problems arise when mainstream workers are not convinced about equal opportunities and deny equal opportunities to disabled children. They can choose to be not very helpful when our staff need support. They do not realise that when we ask them to take a disabled child, we're not talking about Tiny Tim in a wheelchair, but often about difficult young people. If they do not want to accept a child they turn, very quickly, to health and safety issues as a way out. Commercial schemes are reluctant to take disabled children at the price which we are able to pay.
>
> (Co-ordinator, voluntary sector)

Mainstream provision which purports to provide for disabled children may not in fact always do so. This was found to be the case among some services identified as 'inclusive', for the sake of the research, whether by the local authority or by the service's own publicity material. Sometimes the intention to be inclusive was aspirational, merely, without any practical measures to make the service available to disabled children. Informants occasionally expressed a suspicion that some services describe themselves as inclusive as a matter of course, in order to fulfil the criteria required to secure funding. In other cases, providers designate children as disabled when they have special educational needs, rather than disabilities as recognised by social services. For example, some services admit children who are described, informally perhaps, by school or play service staff, as having behavioural difficulties and, on this basis, see themselves as catering for disabled children. This understanding can 'muddy the water' when it come to assessing whether or not mainstream providers do in fact provide an inclusive service when their own account is the sole basis for this assessment. Nevertheless, such a response is perhaps understandable from the view of the service providers. For them, there is in one major sense little difference between physical or sensory impairment and behavioural disorders. In both cases, they perceive a child who will require additional input from staff and thus will have possibly detrimental consequences for the service and for other users. Neither social inclusivity nor children described as 'in need' by the Children Act 1989 are their main concern.

Rationing places

Places available to disabled children are limited and almost always rationed in terms of how many sessions a child may attend, including in special services. For example, in one London Borough social services paid for up to 25 sessions, for each child involved, per year. In part, rationing reflects budgeting priorities and the cost of increased staffing needed for some disabled children. However, few local authorities' budgets could cover children's full participation in play services. One out-of-school services co-ordinator in the North of England estimated that to provide for one child, full time, after school and in the holidays would cost £4,000, a third of her total budget. It is rare that parents can themselves afford the full costs of a place for a disabled child. For non-disabled children, however, such stringent rationing is rare – in part because the cost of provision for them is lower (extra staffing is not required) and in part because their parents are more likely to be employed and therefore to afford to pay the 'going rate' for provision.

Services for members of minority ethnic groups

While places for disabled children and young people in out-of-school services may be limited, two groups seem to be at an even greater disadvantage. These are young people of secondary school age and those whose families belong to a minority ethnic group.

With notable exceptions, service users did not represent the ethnic mix of the local community and children of South Asian background were particularly absent. The situation was less marked in local authorities that had developed a policy towards play which aimed for the inclusion of all children, whatever their disability status or ethnic background. This finding is in keeping with earlier work (Petrie *et al*, 2000), which found that varied interconnected difficulties may underlie the unequal use of services, ranging from the operation of structural racism within services, a lack of training and awareness among staff and providers, the absence of a developed equal opportunities/antiracist policy, lack of monitoring of service users by ethnic group, and a failure to address potential users in the languages relevant to the locality.

Young people aged over 12 years

Inclusive play and care services may be less suitable for young people entering their teens than they are for younger children. Although services may state that they take children up to the age of 13 or 14 years, in effect they are used more generally by children up to the age of 11 or 12 years. Because of this, in conventional play settings older disabled children can find themselves isolated from others because of their age as well as the social disadvantage attached to impairment. Other forms of youth provision may provide more suitable opportunities. For example, a 14-year-old girl in a wheelchair was looking forward to attending summer-school cookery classes again the following year. Because she was three years older than the rest of the class, she had been invited to attend the following year as a 'helper', but had declined, preferring to continue as a student.

In several areas, personal assistant schemes were being established to offer a more flexible type of youth leisure provision. An assistant (sometimes called a befriender) could, for example, accompany a disabled young person to swimming, the cinema, shopping and to mainstream youth provision.

Nevertheless, while some voluntary sector agencies are developing inclusive youth services, and mainstream childcare services for non-disabled secondary school students, up to the age of 14, is a current DfES priority, these services are much rarer than play services. In addition, there has been some cutting back on publicly funded mainstream youth services. In any case youth services do not usually provide a sufficient basis for parents who need full daycare for their children.

3 | The necessary infrastructure for inclusive play

Although there has been some development of inclusive play services, a range of underlying conditions must be met before they can be widespread and satisfactory. A number of underlying structural problems were identified that can hamper the development of mainstream services into inclusive services. Among these were funding, staffing and training, premises, the provision and availability of information, and the provision of transport.

Given adequate staff training and support, and good premises, most experienced informants told us that there is no special mystery about working with disabled children. Indeed, it was common for us, as researchers, to be challenged to identify the disabled children playing among others. After a little experience, staff are said to take inclusive play in their stride and while premises should be generally adequate, it is rarely necessary to make major adaptations for disabled children. Moreover, in some quarters there was a belief that some service providers hide behind the lack of wheelchair accessibility as a reason for not taking disabled children.

Funding for staff

In spite of government action, out-of-school services in general are still in need of development, both in terms of numbers, staffing and practice. Funding issues can be to the fore in all of these areas. It is commonplace for service providers to speak of the problems they meet in continuing to provide their service, irrespective of the inclusion of disabled children. Funding for services is frequently on a one-off basis – whether this is obtained through the New Opportunities Fund, the local authority or other sources. In some cases, we found that a few weeks before the summer holiday, playscheme providers still did not know if they would be able to open because funding decisions were not finalised. They were not, therefore, in a position to complete tasks such as police checks on staff in sufficient time.

The funding of additional support workers for disabled children can suffer from similar timing problems. In at least two local authorities visited, confirmation of funding came too late for service co-ordinators to utilise the funds to support the attendance of disabled children.

One play co-ordinator summed up the situation thus:

> If a child needs one-to-one support then I think we need to provide it because it's not right that staff should be really pushed and taken away to look after one and leave the others because they need to have the right number. That's what play should be about, you need to have the right number of staff and if the club can't afford it then funding or something should be provided for that. I think places like us should be encouraged to do that, and that means not just being told 'you should be providing inclusive play', but 'here is the means to do that'. Otherwise you're asking people to do what perhaps

they can't do. There needs to be more training available, there needs to be more funding available for it. We've got to show we're committed to it, so the children can grow up in that environment.

Workers are often employed on a temporary part-time basis. Except in some local authority provision that is open all year round, pay is often low considering the responsibilities involved in the work. In the opinion of a representative of the DfES, this is likely to be the case for the near future.[1] It is not surprising that the workforce for out-of-school services may at present be characterised as somewhat underdeveloped, although organisations such as SPRITO (National Training Organisation for Sports Recreation and Allied Industries), the National Centres for Playwork Education, and Kids Clubs Network are active in increasing and improving opportunities for training and qualification.

When funding is precarious, the support and development of the staff team is also difficult, and continuity of employment and the development of an experienced and trained workforce becomes an important issue. All staff, not just a 'key worker', need training in order to provide the support required for disabled children (see p. 22). Apart from considerations of good practice, training can allay the fears and insecurities of staff with no previous knowledge of disabled children. One play leader observed:

> I think a lot of play projects don't take children with special needs because they don't understand what the need is. Therefore they need factual information about various conditions, syndromes, and ways of handling things so that they are more secure in what they need. I think a lot of them are just scared to take these children in case something goes wrong.

One local authority play co-ordinator observed that the training most playschemes requested was preparation for specific conditions, such as how to work with children with autism, the preparation of staff to work with children with ADHD and how to physically handle children with limited mobility.

The development of training courses needs funding and staff need to be paid to undertake courses in what would otherwise be their own time. Temporary staff, employed to meet the extra demands of the summer holiday, also need an element of training for work with disabled children. Training and team development should be seen as part of the necessary underpinning of all out-of-school services, benefiting (and protecting) disabled and non-disabled children alike; in addition there needs to be a component of training that identifies the key objectives of inclusive play and how these are to be achieved. A playworker said:

> It's about attitudes and it's training staff to look out for areas where their actions might hinder integration. And that might be something as simple as setting up an activity that involves, I don't know, climbing a tree for instance. Not everybody in the group could take part in that. So it's training staff to think creatively when they design activities.

Many out of-school services rely on volunteers for staffing, in an attempt to reduce costs whilst maintaining adequate staffing cover. One co-ordinator for a national charity, who led a county-wide out-of-school inclusion project, observed that volunteers were becoming harder to find. To offer good support they needed training, but time for this raised problems regarding work rotas. This charity had almost entirely stopped using volunteers as support staff. Its staff believed that good support requires good preparation and good note-keeping, which it was unreasonable to expect volunteers to undertake in their own time, in addition to their contact time with children.

Premises and accommodation

Reversed integration services are often sited in facilities which are specially adapted for disabled children. However, mainstream schemes operate in a range of locations, with varying degrees of suitability. We saw, in this as in other studies, services making use of premises that appeared inadequate for non-disabled children, let alone for any with mobility and communication difficulties. As one play leader observed:

> Yes, we've got wheelchair access but the steps are broken. A wheelchair might be all right, but able bodied might fall up the stairs. . . .We did do a risk assessment, but we decided that because the building is a temporary home for us, we couldn't do too much about it. All we could do was minimise the real risks and eliminate the potential risks, if you like, like the steps. But the real risks, like with glass and that, we had to deal with.

Included in the services visited were those with little or no outdoor play space, or outdoor space which afforded no shelter from sun or rain. Cramped indoor facilities sometimes required children to be organised in a programme of highly structured activities, rather than providing opportunity for free play. In some buildings there was no separate area where children might withdraw for quiet play while in others parts of the building were inaccessible for wheelchair users.

Inadequate indoor premises present problems especially when rain limits outdoor activity. This can cause concern about the safety of children with limited mobility in a cramped space. Services are forced to take this into consideration and may resort to rationing places for children with disabilities when physical space is limited.

In reverse integration services, we saw full and accessible facilities for washing and changing disabled children. In some of the mainstream services visited, the toilets and washing facilities were generally inadequate, let alone suitable for use with disabled children. In some services, there were too few toilets, a lack of hot water, soap and towels. Toilets were in some cases dirty and not cleaned frequently. Without proper facilities workers did what they could to care for children. In one case, an 8-year-old child was cleansed standing in a wash hand basin, in front of other children. This showed little respect for his dignity, but was seen as the best of poor options. In this case, the toilet facilities were shared with other groups using the same building and other users complained about the practice on the grounds of hygiene (see also pp. 29–30).

Information on inclusive play

The parents of disabled school-age children may have specific difficulties when it comes to finding out about services. Before children start school, local networks can be a source of information on a variety of resources. But, when children start school at some distance from the family home or in a different local authority, local networks are weakened. Also, teachers and social workers are not necessarily aware of available provision and services may not advertise because places fill up quickly enough without advertisement.[2] Ways of making information readily accessible, between local authorities and across departments, still need to be identified, even in areas where there is some developed policy towards inclusive play. Providing proper information for the parents of disabled children is an objective of the Quality Protects programme.[3]

Transport

The provision of transport to take children to and from services can be of vital importance in facilitating access to out-of-school services. It is also important that parents know about the availability of transport, otherwise they may not even explore the use of a service. The use of public transport presents practical difficulties for some parents, while taxis are expensive and do not always provide good physical access. Yet, in some local authorities, transport is only provided for children with extreme physical difficulties. At present, disabled children are more likely to attend holiday playschemes than after-school clubs, partly because transport problems seem to be more frequently addressed during school holidays. Yet, in the evening, children attending special schools or units may require additional transport if they are to attend mainstream after-school clubs in the neighbourhood where the family lives. Transport is needed to take a child from school to an after-school club and later, if necessary, to take them home. In at least one local authority visited, after-school transport was not consistently provided to out-of-school services and appeared dependent on the flexibility of a particular transport provider and whether they were prepared to undertake the journey involved.

1. Nick Tooze, speaking at *Check This Out! Meeting the Needs of Young People 8–14 Years*, National Conference, London 21 September, 2000.
2. There are two routes into provision: one through a direct approach by parents, the other via local authority, social services, heath professionals or voluntary agency personnel.
3. Objective 6.4.

4 Developing the infrastructure for inclusive play

How can out-of-school services be supported in their development towards inclusivity? From the evidence of this and earlier work, it is clear that individual out-of-school services are not in a strong position to develop inclusive play without additional support, whether for the funding of extra staff, the provision of training or the development of outreach work with families. Neither are the parents of disabled children likely to be in a position to contribute substantially to the development of services. Many are unemployed, or the family may rely on one income only – the parents of disabled children are less likely to be in paid work than other parents (Thomas *et al.*, 1994). Needing more material resources than others they are less able to pay either the market rate for services or for any extra costs that occur in providing for their child such as extra staffing (Beresford, 1995: 14).

In this section we look at the role of the local authority and voluntary agencies in supporting the development of inclusive play.

Local authority play services support

Some local authorities have a written play policy that includes support for inclusive play, but where there is little in the way of local play development, inclusive play is more difficult to provide.

We found evidence that local authority play services, where they exist, were attempting to provide for disabled children. For example in one London borough, where local authority play facilities are all based on a day-care model and rely to some extent on the fees of working parents, the authority provides places for children in need (including disabled children) whose parents are unemployed. This same borough, and other local authorities with a developed play policy, supplies the necessary infrastructure for inclusive play through its general support for play and care services. Such support can, for example, include: a developed play policy for all children that gives consideration to disabled children as a special group; the employment of play officers; the designation of named personnel with overall responsibility for play services for disabled children.

Other local authorities, while not themselves providing play or care services, support community play providers. For example, they fund the employment of play co-ordinators in the voluntary sector and provide other grant aid to services. They may insist on provision being inclusive as a condition of grant aid or of local authority support for funding applications.

A developed and implemented local play policy can in itself be a firm foundation for inclusive play. For example, Stirling council's play service provides a range of co-ordinated play opportunities: summer events (for example circus skills weeks and other activities in parks and on housing estates), and a soft playroom within one community centre, available for all local playschemes and after-school clubs. It brings in the resources of the local museum and of wildlife experts as additional resources for services and aims to make children's unsupervised play areas in local parks as interesting as possible. This it does in consultation with children – including disabled children. The school-age care network is co-ordinated and supported from the same base and there are strong links with a voluntary sector organisation which promotes and facilitates inclusive play (see Playplus, p. 18), so that disabled children can be included in play opportunities.

Funding by social services

The Children Act 1989 encourages the deployment of resources for families with children in need, including those with disabled children. Out-of-school holiday services are mentioned specifically. We found that sometimes 'spot funding', as permitted under Section 17 of the Children Act, followed the child to meet any additional staffing needed in out-of-school placements. In other cases, social services had established a service agreement with a particular provider to provide places for disabled children. One London authority was using carers' grants to support play services for all work with disabled children. Elsewhere, social services funded one-to-one workers, whether employed by a voluntary agency or directly by the playscheme itself.

In a local authority in west London, the education department had been funding a voluntary sector adventure playground project. This precluded the voluntary organisation from obtaining money from another department in the same authority. Social services, therefore, funded individual children to attend (as permitted under used Section 17 of the Children Act) rather than grant-aiding the organisation to provide the service. Here, the money was used to pay for a one-to-one worker. The same department used part of the local authority carer's grant to provide families with home-based respite care, and play services. Because this was still not enough to cover costs, the extent to which parents should contribute had become a somewhat contentious issue. The parents of disabled children claimed that because there was no charge made for non-disabled children to attend the playscheme, their children, also, should attend free of charge. Social services were deliberating whether parents should be asked to contribute out of the disabled living allowance. All of these difficulties demonstrate the conflicts arising when issues of justice and inclusion are dealt with in the context of limited resources.

Voluntary sector and early years partnership support

EYDCPs (Early Years and Care Development Partnerships) represent the interests of local authority and voluntary sector in children and childcare. Thus, they have a part to play in supporting and promoting inclusive play. Their remit to develop out-of-school services means that, potentially, they are influential. It was reported in one area that the EYDCP insisted that all out-of-school schemes seeking funding should have a designated and trained person with responsibility for inclusive practice. Elsewhere, it was reported that the partnerships do not as yet necessarily give consideration to inclusive play and care, in spite of the Disability Discrimination Act 1995 and its insistence that from December 1996:

> Service providers must not discriminate against disabled people (including children) by refusing to provide any service which is provided to members of the public, providing a lower standard of service or offering a service on less favourable terms.
>
> (DfEE, 2001: 15)

Voluntary organisations

Local and national voluntary organisations can support inclusive play, through advocacy, supplying training and resources, local co-ordination, and putting families in touch with services. To illustrate the diversity of their involvement, we will describe in some detail three local organisations that are dedicated to the development of inclusive services.

Parasol

Parasol is a voluntary agency, started by Oxford social services and the youth service, initially to provide a youth club for children with disabilities. Its aim now is to facilitate inclusive play throughout Oxfordshire. Parasol has a co-ordinator, an administrative assistant and an outreach worker. Its funding comes from Oxfordshire social services, Oxford City Council Leisure Services (where it has strong links with the play development officer) and the National Charities Lottery Board. Social services conduct and pay for the police checks on Parasol's 'enablers', who work directly with disabled children. Four or five enablers are recruited for term-time and about twelve for the summer holiday. Enablers are employed by play providers at around £5.50 per hour. In the first instance, parents approach Parasol and register with them. A suitable playscheme or after-school club is identified and arrangements are made for the enabler to be employed by the playscheme. The child's support needs at the out-of-school services are identified, based on visits to their home and/or school.

Parasol tries to reach the different minority ethnic communities in Oxfordshire. It also monitors the children it works with to see if different ethnic groups are properly represented. However, Parasol believes that it is still not supporting sufficient children from Chinese and Asian groups.

Over time Parasol aims to become a training and development agency for inclusive play and care rather than just a supplier of 'enablers', in the belief that services can themselves identify what is needed, especially when parents make a direct approach for a place. The co-ordinator of Parasol said 'We have to help them think how they can best support a child'.

Playplus

Stirling council's children's services combine, in the same Children's Services Department, education, social services, play and out-of-school care services. The department relates closely to a voluntary project, Playplus, which has developed over 14 years. Playplus promotes inclusive play and leisure for children and young people aged 5 to 19 years who have physical and learning disabilities. Core funding comes from Children's Services, and Playplus works in partnership with play and out-of-school childcare. It enables disabled children to attend play projects in their local communities. It trains playworkers in inclusive issues and supplies playworkers as members of staff in mainstream provision. It also operates a 'befrienders' scheme by which paid members of staff take children on individual outings and facilitate their participation in playschemes and other leisure opportunities. It runs youth services and projects.

Each Stirling playscheme has, as well as a senior worker, a Playplus co-ordinator to co-ordinate and oversee work with disabled children (although their interactions with children on site are far from confined to disabled children). This is in addition to any staff needed to increase the staffing ratio for work with disabled children.

There is also some spot purchasing of places on playschemes by social services. Playplus is happy for social workers to pass on information about playschemes to parents of disabled children and to Playplus staff. However, Playplus and the Stirling play service personnel believe that children should be included in play and out-of-school services only after there has been discussion with parents and children as to the suitability of any particular service and the child's needs and wishes. They do not see it as appropriate that social workers should refer children to playschemes.

Playplus holds a database of playworkers and befrienders, known to them over years. Many befrienders are students at the local university who were pleased to be involved on an *ad hoc* basis. At the time of the research they were paid a little over £6 per hour, somewhat higher than the rate for workers on playschemes.

IPOP

IPOP is an independent organisation that developed out of Barnet Play Association. Its aim is to support play opportunities for children with disabilities and to raise awareness of the benefits of inclusive provision both in play settings and more widely. Their brochure states that 'Healthy communities include everyone and all children benefit from playing together in an environment which offers the same opportunities to everyone'.

For each disabled child, IPOP provides a one-to-one support worker. The worker gets to know the family and child and works alongside the child, in the service that best suits the child and the family's needs. After a 12-week settling-in period, the family must contact the social services' children with disabilities team, and ask them to refer the family back to IPOP, with funding for a full-time support worker.

A typical arrangement is for a child to have an agreed 'plan' to attend an after-school scheme or youth club, with one or two sessions per child per week being supported, and similarly for a youth club. Plans cover 25 days of support per year. In 2000, IPOP charged social services £6.50 per hour for supplying a support worker, and an additional element to cover their own core costs.

National organisations

Kidsactive

Kidsactive is a national charity, established in 1966, which promotes play for disabled children and campaigns for equal access to play opportunities for all children. It manages a training and information service. Kidsactive runs six adventure playgrounds in London offering play to disabled children, including some services based on 'reversed integration'. It also offers training and consultancy services, nationally.

Barnado's

Alongside its other work, Barnado's facilitates play for disabled children. For example, in Somerset an inclusion officer visits families and completes a standard form on the child's needs. This information is passed on to the service to be consulted as necessary.

National Children's Homes and Mencap

The National Children's Homes and Mencap are other examples of national organisations involved in the field.

5 Practice within inclusive play services

In this section, we look at practice that can enable disabled children to get the most out of play services. It covers examining arrangements in advance of use, so as to provide the best opportunity for children to settle in well, and to enjoy themselves and the companionship of other children. It also looks at referrals, choice of service, extra staffing requirements, communication between parents, children and staff, play and risk, working with challenging behaviour, and issues such as lifting and carrying, hygiene and personal care, and administering medicines.

Referrals

In more than one local authority, social workers were discouraged by local authority or voluntary sector co-ordinators from referring a child directly to a playscheme, without all those concerned meeting in advance. Choosing the right service for a child was seen as needing the prior involvement of the play staff and the family if it was to be successful. There were cases reported where a social worker, in order to obtain a place, presented an incomplete account of the support that a child needed. This had led to parents bringing their child to a scheme that lacked the washing facilities that the child required, and the service provider having reluctantly to explain to the disappointed parents that the child could not be accommodated. Some service providers were concerned that social workers did not foresee the need to arrange a place for a child ahead of the summer holiday (for example, in a both a northern area and in the Midlands). When this happened and where a child required additional attention, staffing difficulties could occur: sometimes it was impossible to include a child in a scheme because additional staffing was not available at short notice. A play leader described a situation when a child came with inadequate preparation.

> The first week he came in with his [registration] forms that he had. No disability [was mentioned]. It became blatantly obvious, as soon as he came through the door that he did have special needs, so we discussed with parents, the social worker, what this child's needs were, [and preparations were] put in place for the following weeks.

Prior to a child's admission, the suitability of a particular service should be assessed. Practice encountered by the research team (especially where there was the involvement of voluntary sector organisations, such as those described in the last section) included visits by staff to the child's home and school to provide a better understanding of the child's needs and any extra support required. Parents and children were also invited to visit a service during opening hours, to see what was on offer and ascertain what was needed to prepare the child. In some cases parents remained on site during a settling-in period. A mother said:

You know you have to take time to be with your child at those schemes, until you're really happy about it. I mean I certainly did with Tom when he started coming on the Saturday playscheme until I was really sure that he was integrating with, I mean, I haven't any question about how people look after him but I just wanted to make sure that he was relating to them, that he felt comfortable there.

The usual procedures for taking contact numbers, and signing consent forms in case a child needs medical treatment, were followed by all services. The following represents the most developed practice encountered:

The senior member of staff asks the child and the parents about the child's likes, dislikes and any special requirements regarding food or activities. They find out essential information regarding how the child communicates and, if the child communicates through signs, what are the most useful signs for staff to know. They enquire if the child has a way of requesting the toilet, or if this needs to be suggested and at what intervals. Where appropriate, staff find out about mobility aids, and the correct use of these; whether children wear e.g. safety helmets and knee pads; any medication to be given routinely, or in specific circumstances. A record of all of the above is made accessible to all staff and volunteers and regularly updated.

Special preparation may be necessary where a child has language difficulties. Staff can nevertheless be alert to the needs and wishes of the child. This involves being attentive to means other than those of spoken language, such as the child's emotional state as conveyed through facial expression, body language or sounds. Some services have more developed understandings and practice in this respect than others. At one summer playscheme, run by a national voluntary organisation, the child *as a person* is placed, consciously, at the forefront of practice. Here, a senior worker said that it was important to make a presumption of an intelligent emotional life for all the children, and went on to say that children's feelings are evident from their expressions and actions – which staff should respond to. Another worker on the same site said that this was perhaps the only setting where children were not constantly meeting other people's requirements: 'It is beautiful when a child realises that this is their choice, what they do. Their whole body language expresses relief.'

Staff need also to be aware of each child's capabilities so that they can ensure that children not overprotected but allowed to take as full a part in play as possible. Issues surrounding safety, adventurous play and risk management are discussed below.

Brothers and sisters

Disabled children can have a positive relationship with their brothers and sisters that can be a model for other children. Nevertheless, providers sometimes found it necessary to give special consideration to the sibling of a disabled child attending the same service. They thought that in some cases a brother or sister might take a lot of responsibility for the disabled child, at home. So they judged if, and how, they might relieve them of some of this responsibility, within the service; they expressed this in terms of siblings having the right to play and not always finding themselves in the position of carers (we do not know what the brothers and sisters thought, although our earlier research suggested that some parents had concerns on this issue). One playscheme apportioned time for a pair of siblings so that they attended together on one day to enable their mother to have a break, and each attended singly on other days. This gave the brothers a break from each other both at home and at the playscheme.

Staffing

There was varied practice regarding the appointment and deployment of staff to work with disabled children. Properly, decisions about this ought to be made before a particular child starts attending. Some services may decide that a child with more serious disabilities should be supported, one to one, by a key worker employed in addition to existing staff. Such a person might, for example, take particular responsibility for toileting, feeding and the administration of medicines. S/he may also be required to carry out procedures such as feeding through a gastro-nasal or gastric tube. However, in other services it was seen as necessary only to supplement the staff group by an extra worker, with responsibility for the disabled child, but not necessarily maintaining immediate proximity with that child. In yet other services, responsibility for the child was spread throughout the staff group – although this may be augmented by an extra member of staff when the disabled child attends. A member of staff on a playscheme commented:

> Everybody is aware that there's children that receive one to one and that that isn't . . . that shouldn't be implemented in a sort of ball and chain type of way and that the aspiration is to give the children as much independent play as possible. So there are times when even one-to-one children don't need it.

As we say elsewhere in this report, extra staffing can sometimes act as a buffer between the disabled child and others. Indeed, some playschemes limit the number of children requiring more than the standard ratio of staffing in order to ensure a satisfactory balance in the numbers of adults and children present. They believe that 'too many adults' may be inimical to a play ethos. As members of staff gain experience and confidence in dealing with children with specific disabilities, they can sometimes operate without additional support workers. Whilst a child may start by needing a designated worker, one to one, in time this need can decline as all staff learn to work with the child who, at the same time, is becoming accustomed to the provision.

But longstanding experience does not obviate the need for ongoing training. It is not only new staff and volunteers who may have to be reminded about showing respect for disabled children. In one well-established service, where the researcher was talking to a group of children, staff came and wheeled some individuals away, without explanation to the child, the researcher or the other children in the group. In another setting, which had also had inclusive play for many years, the senior worker described how staff had discussed at length the implications for the feelings and dignity of all the children present when a playworker shouted out 'It's time for N's rectal Valium', and that this had been a learning point for issues of children's privacy.

Staff in one playscheme felt themselves to be particularly disadvantaged when dealing with children with disabilities because of the lack of training provided:

> We haven't got any specialised equipment, we haven't got any training, I mean, J., she's gone on a few workshops but that, we haven't had . . . we haven't had any really practical advice to tell you the truth. We just haven't. . . . Because if a child has a massive temper tantrum, I'm not quite sure how to diffuse the situation. And we do our best and I don't know whether it's right or wrong.

These were workers who were doing their best to provide inclusive play, but their good will was undermined because their professional development was not supported.

Non-disabled children

Where there has previously been no other disabled child attending a scheme, non-disabled children may need to be prepared in advance for their new companion. Some services made a point of displaying positive images of disabled people, or providing books that gave child-friendly information about impairments. Disabled adults were sometimes (albeit rarely) employed as staff. This, too, was seen as removing some of the stigma surrounding impairment.

With familiarity and explanation, children can learn to have concern for each other. At one scheme, when a new child entrant first had an epileptic fit, this had led to the other children crowding round to see what was happening. The play leaders explained carefully to the children what had occurred so that when a seizure recurred (as it did frequently) the other children knew what was happening and took no excessive interest. However, during the recovery periods they checked, caringly, that the girl was progressing and asked when she would be rejoining them in their activity. Preparation is all-important, as one of the staff involved said:

> I think integration's very good for them but I think there are other occasions when children who aren't familiar with disabled children can be rather nasty to them, it's a question of them being educated.

One senior playworker recalled the difficulties regarding the settling in of one child with behavioural difficulties:

> By the end of the first week that A was here, he had calmed down a bit, because obviously he'd begun to know our routine a little bit. But the other children were a bit frightened of him, which is a little bit sad.

It takes skill and experience on the part of staff to ensure that the outcomes of difficulties are positive, and that children do not become prejudiced against disabled people. Services need to develop means of introducing disabled children to others in ways that are likely to lead to their inclusion in play and friendship groups.

Those appointed as support staff can be responsible not only for the child's physical and emotional wellbeing but for ensuring that, in most circumstances, disabled and non-disabled children interact. They should also be aware that they themselves may create a physical or psychological barrier between their charges and other children, and should take steps to see that this does not happen. If they are always too close to the child or are over-protective, then children may be less likely to make overtures to each other.

Inclusive play sometimes needs the direct intervention of staff to ensure that activities include the disabled child. For example, staff can find innovative ways of including children in favoured activities. Staff in a reversed integration playscheme would only allow the computer room to be used if a disabled child was taking part. Other staff devised games which provided 'a level playing field', such as a shuffle football in which all players remained seated on the ground. They suggested special conditions such as, in a game of cricket, a child in a wheelchair bats and another person takes the runs. It seems likely that such practice helps children to get to know one another so that, later, they interact on their own initiative; nevertheless staff need to be skilled in order to ensure that these strategies do not 'backfire' – they can only be successful if they are done in the spirit of play and all children enjoy them.

One service used a 'buddy' system, where a particular child volunteers to help the disabled child to settle in. However, preparing children may be more difficult where children – disabled or otherwise – do not attend regularly or very frequently. In these cases, the formation of stable friendship groups can be more difficult.

For children with more profound and complex disabilities, and conditions such as autism, sharing the same play space may be as much as can be achieved. Nevertheless, disabled children do not have to be passive bystanders to other children's play.

> At Green Fields, the children with more profound disabilities were constantly accompanied by a member of staff. For example, a child in a wheelchair, and without language, might be assigned a key worker for a morning. The member of staff would sit with the child or wheel them about; the couple often became a social focus for other ambulant children, disabled or not. The other children might sit and chat with the member of staff and with one another, or play word games, tell jokes, plait each other's hair or just play close at hand. In such cases the child in the wheelchair might be a social participant, to whom remarks were addressed, or objects shown and who made their own contribution to interactions. On other occasions, a child in a wheelchair might be allocated – or undertake – a more passive role, such as that of an onlooker who showed interest but was not included or did not participate; still others might not react at all to the activities of other children.
>
> (Petrie *et al.*, 2000: 78)

Monitoring and reviewing

Experienced staff and play officers thought that monitoring children's welfare was important, both when they first started to attend a play service and thereafter. Children and services both change over time. Life events, such as spells in hospital, may change how a child reacts to a service; their level of mobility can change; friends may leave; some seasonal (or commercial) activities among other children may tend to be more excluding than others. All such circumstance must be addressed. Parents, too, should be consulted as to their understanding of how the child is getting on, and children's own wishes and dissatisfactions should be listened to. Regular monitoring as part of a service's regular activities, means that problems can be nipped in the bud so that children benefit fully from what the service has to offer.

Communication within the staff group

Good communication among staff is always important and especially so regarding disabled children. In some services, the communication of necessary information was conducted informally and did not result in all those concerned being properly briefed. In others, relevant information from parents was passed on to the whole staff group, including sessional staff and volunteers. It may be important that staff know, for example, that a child has had a bad night, or that workers tell one another about incidents (such as signs of unhappiness) which have occurred. Some services made a feature of daily staff meetings to discuss how children were getting on and to plan accordingly. Setting aside time for a short daily staff meeting, while desirable, requires that staff be paid for this time over and above their face-to-face work with children. This may be beyond the resources of under-funded provision although many services described the clearing-up time at the end of the day as a valuable time when they discussed issues which had arisen over the course of the day, whilst they tidied and prepared for the following session.

Communicating with parents

Communicating with parents about their child's experience can be especially important in the case of children who cannot themselves describe their play-scheme experience to their parents. A mother said:

> My daughter, who couldn't, my younger one, who couldn't speak at the time, obviously hated it and for about a week or two weeks after that if we ever went to a bus stop she would sort of really tense up because she was frightened I was going to take her to this place but I never knew what, what it was that she didn't like.

If a child is having a difficult time settling in, this should be discussed with parents, who may be able to cast some light on what is the matter and how to proceed. It should not be left to the parent to have to guess that something is wrong from their child's demeanour. It may be helpful to say to parents, before the child starts and without being overly negative, that should any problems arise they will be addressed jointly by staff and parents.

A reliance on written communication may not be sufficiently personal for parents who are anxious about leaving their child in an unfamiliar situation. One scheme in the West of England had developed a pro forma to be completed by staff and given to parents when they came to collect children. It gave details of the child's activities and anything that needed to be brought to the parents' notice. The local social service department, however, was said to view this procedure as discriminating against disabled children, because all children did not have such a report. Perhaps more importantly, a pro forma is a 'blunt instrument' when it comes to passing on potentially sensitive information and cannot do justice to the complexities of children's experience.

Some staff may, instinctively, communicate well, but this is not something that can be left to chance:

> All staff need training, down to the person who is answering the phone, if they are to interact appropriately with parents and children.
>
> (Local authority play co-ordinator)

There may be practical communication difficulties when a child is not accompanied by their parent to and from the service, but is taken on special transport. Where this happens, staff will need to find other ways of communicating with parents. For some, the telephone is the most usual means of communication. Staff may need to phone parents to alert them to anything untoward and to ask for advice, for example, about medication when a child is experiencing epileptic seizures. Or it may be that staff want to get in touch just to tell the parent how the child has enjoyed the day.

For their part, parents often commented that staff should be encouraged to tell parents about the more positive aspect of the child's experience as well as discussing any difficulties. They thought that the discussion of difficulties should be handled judiciously, avoiding any suggestion of blame regarding the child or the parent. Incidents were reported where the parent thought that some staff did not understood the nature of the child's impairment and were critical of behaviour that the parent saw as being outside the child's control.

> The staff complained about N. when we came to pick him up in the evening and said things like 'He's been bad, bad, bad, today' or 'He shouted a lot, he pinched people'.

A London mother revealed something of the hurt that parents experience:

> Inclusion is all very well when they're younger, aged 5, 6 or 7, then they can go to after-school scheme or playgroup. But after that they become less cute, people don't like a dribbly teenager.

It is important that staff do not add to parents' sense of exclusion, that they understand that parents cannot be held responsible for children's behaviour, and that 'blaming' them is hurtful and unlikely to help either the parent or the child. For this reason too, it is important to tell parents about the positive aspects of a child's time while using a service.

Challenging behaviour

Some services develop, in advance of need, ways of reacting to challenging behaviour presented by non-disabled and disabled children. Staff are, therefore, prepared to react in a considered way when difficulties present. Of special importance is the preparation for staff on how to react to discriminatory remarks and behaviour by non-disabled children towards other children. Children's meetings and 'circle time' can provide an occasion for discussing this and for talking about respect for diversity, generally. Workers also told us that if a child made disparaging remarks they should be taken to one side and told that the disabled child could be hurt by their behaviour.

Although staff often said words to the effect that children 'don't think twice about a child with special needs', it should not be assumed that disabled children are always accepted by others, even in services with well-established practices towards inclusive play. For example, in a reversed integration setting, with a long history of inclusive play, non-disabled children were seen to reject a disabled child from their den on the grounds that 'this is only for people who can talk properly'. Her one-to-one worker remonstrated with the children and said 'Anyone can play with anyone here'. However the children insisted 'This is only for people who can talk. Only people who can talk properly can come into our house'. The disabled child and her worker eventually moved away. This example is given because it highlights the competing values which underlie respect for the dynamics of free play on the one hand and inclusive play on the other. This is an issue which could provide fruitful discussion in staff meetings and in training.

'Getting away' with unacceptable behaviour

Staff in mainstream services told us that, with explanation, non-disabled children understand and do not have a problem when some disabled children behave somewhat differently from themselves. That said, staff should be prepared for other children to accuse them of sometimes letting children with learning difficulties 'get away with' unacceptable behaviour. In this and in the earlier study, we found that for some staff this was a difficult area. There could be tensions between staff who felt that all children were 'the same' and should be treated the same, and those who thought that allowances should be made in some cases. A senior worker from the West of England echoed some of the ambivalence that untrained staff might feel:

> There was a little bit of friction between the staff, because some of them said, 'Oh he's great. He's managed to restrain himself from punching a little 4-year-old tot in the face.' And the other staff said, 'But he shouldn't be doing it anyway, you know.'

Also, although children 'telling tales' or complaining about disabled children was discouraged, staff in a Midlands summer playscheme said that it could be acceptable when behaviour was dangerous, or even when it was 'inappropriate'. She cited a child who took his clothes off in the garden.

Working with challenging behaviour

Some of the difficulty experienced by staff around children's behaviour derived from the fact that, because places were rationed, staff and children sometimes did not have sufficient time to get to know each other. The implication was that, without rationing and with more frequent attendance, there might be fewer difficulties in this area.

Staff used a variety of means of understanding and working with challenging behaviour. In one service, for example, it was seen primarily as a means by which children communicated their feelings. It was basically an 'optimistic event', by which they attempted to gain control over their lives and as such needed understanding and working with. Other services made a point of finding out how the challenging behaviour displayed by a particular disabled child was dealt with at home and at school, and then considering how appropriate this was for a *play* setting; they also considered the child's needs for consistency. At other times, diversionary tactics were employed, or staff resorted to the use of conditions: 'We try to say 'If you're good for one hour you can come to the park' rather than 'If you're bad you won't come'.

> Autistic children have to learn how to behave in an acceptable way. Yes, it is challenging for them to go on the tube, but they have a good time. Now we're helping some to move on to a youth centre. These people have been separated from the world and it makes the world a poorer place. But a lot of 6-year-olds in the playschemes could give a lesson on autism, because they've seen it and understand – they know why a child is 'in a paddy' – it's because he's scared, because his routine has been interrupted
>
> (Co-ordinator, Voluntary Sector, London)

Nevertheless, the behaviour of some children could pose real difficulties for staff and other children, resulting sometimes in the allocation of one-to-one supervision. This sometimes occurred with the child's knowledge, but sometimes at a distance, without the child being aware of it. In other cases certain children were seen as too violent for others, scaring younger children. Here, a variety of strategies might be adopted:

> First of all we talk to the child and ask how they would they feel about being treated like that. We do this quietly away from other children. We may speak to the parent if we think they ought to know.
>
> (Senior playworker, Midlands)

Throughout the course of the work, there were examples of children who had been asked to leave some schemes but had then gone on to thrive in others. In one such case, a child was passed on to a youth group where he was said to 'get on fine', being the youngest member.

Another service attributed its success with a 9-year-old boy, who had been excluded from another service because of his behaviour, to two factors: the emphasis on talking about the playscheme's rules at circle time, and the range of activity options which prevented children becoming 'trapped' in an activity and becoming bored.

Some services reported excluding children for a session because of unacceptable behaviour.

> We have had problems with a child who was biting other children. On one occasion we had to send him home because it happened twice in one day, and staff felt he did understand, and other children were at risk.
>
> (Senior playworker, mainstream playscheme)

At one playscheme, the behaviour of an older boy towards staff and children in general was frequently aggressive. It was usually regarded as 'just part of him'. However, on one occasion the aggression had become more personalised and directed mainly at one individual and so was felt to be more bullying than usual. As after discussion there had been no improvement, the boy had been excluded for a day and the situation eased.

Staff occasionally said that they had excluded children indefinitely. They recognised that this was upsetting for children and parents; it was also a cause of regret for themselves, especially where there was no one to call on for support or training regarding aggressive behaviour. When boys were involved, staff sometimes felt that they might have dealt with the situation better if male workers had been present – but women outnumber men in play services, although less so than in early years settings.

Communication with the parents of other children could be helpful:

> We explain that safety is our priority. A lot of parents understand that and these things [i.e. aggressive behaviour] can happen in the playground. Here [it] is safer than any-where else in terms of supervision, the numbers of qualified people supervising them. So if a child hurts somebody, we talk to the parents of the other child and we will explain that the child has special needs and we are doing all we can to support them. Generally speaking they are very understanding. They know that their own child is not perfect so, you know, I think we just talk it through the best we can.

However a senior worker in another service perceived situations which might escalate beyond the level that they could cope with. In this case the non-disabled child who had been threatened had a father who was himself seen as aggressive:

> And from my difficulty, the child he kept going for, and it wasn't intentionally, it just happened to this little boy, he happened to be there every time . . . because the father will come down and . . . because he is well known for putting people out. And I said I can't have my staff and myself, because I'm like front line, I'm here and I just can't cope with that. And I was thinking, don't tell his dad, please . . . just, because we're quite vulnerable.

This last extract points to some of the complexities of the playworker's task – complexities for which individuals may have received very little training or ongoing support.

Play and safety

While there were registration officers who were familiar with the play ethos on which some out-of-school services are based, sometimes staff believed that registration officers had little understanding of play facilities and could be over-anxious about children, the sorts of activities in which they might participate, and the swings and climbing equipment available. For example:

> A rough alleyway connects two parts of the site and is in constant use by the children. It is edged with grass, shrubs, overhanging thistles and nettles. The senior worker believes that children should not be protected from these; they should learn about their properties through direct experience. The children do not need adults to oversee every aspect of their safety and comfort. He believes that children are more vulnerable if they are over-dependent upon adults. Within playwork there is a strong tradition that children should be allowed to take risks, in contrast to a more protective ethos often found in other work with children.
>
> (Petrie et al., 2000: 81)

Some play staff believe that young people can only learn how to assess risk through engaging with risk.

Earlier studies suggest that children and parents can be especially appreciative of the opportunities provided for what is seen as 'normal' play, with the mess and scrapes that this may involve.

Risk is not to be ignored, however. A Kidsactive play officer said that playworkers should constantly be aware of the need to assess risk, and should do so in terms of:

- the risk posed by equipment and environment and what can be done to obviate or minimise this, such as setting rules about how many children use a swing at the same time or procedures to be observed at a swimming pool;
- risk which attaches to a particular child – a child who has never used a craft knife needs to be shown how to do so and supervised; a child with behavioural difficulties needs supervision when interacting with other children near a slide.

This sort of risk assessment applies to playwork in general, not just that involving disabled children.

Medicines

In some cases, services adopted local school guidelines for the administration of medicines, and had a formal policy applying to staff and volunteers. For example, in a metropolitan area in the Midlands, each child had a general healthcare plan, which contained, for example, what to do in an emergency or when to call a doctor. This also contained information about medication. A formal request was required from the parent for staff to administer a medicine. Staff were trained about giving medicine and their training was recorded. There was also a record of all medication given. In other services, policy and practice was less formal and staff did not seem to be aware that this might give rise to problems. There were also services where staff refused to administer medicine.

Lifting and carrying

In one of the London areas studied, local authority health and safety officers had raised issues regarding lifting and carrying disabled children. For example, if a child were to fall in the playground they had instructed staff not to lift them without the use of a hoist. The hoist should also be used for toileting. In the same authority, staff believed that this was an insensitive way of dealing with the children and ignored the instruction. They also pointed out that in the majority of inclusive services no hoist is available. They thought that if the purchase of a hoist were to be required by health and safety authorities, this could be a hindrance to opening mainstream services to disabled children.

One service in the Midlands had taken a different approach to lifting. They had asked the health authority for advice on safe lifting and carrying.

Toilets and toileting

With regard to toilets and toileting, three main considerations have arisen in the course of this and other studies: considerations of dignity and respect, hygiene and comfort, and accessibility. Earlier we highlighted how toilets and washing facilities may be inadequate and unhygienic: attention always needs to be given to correcting this.

Workers sometimes reported that children, especially the older ones, preferred a worker of the same sex to accompany them to the toilet and change them. Some senior workers were especially pleased when they were able to obtain the services of male staff. It was also seen as preferable for children to know the worker involved in toileting and that workers should not be seen as interchangeable for this. For example, a mother said that her 13-year-old son, attending a reversed integration playscheme in London, had for a whole day denied needing to be changed. This was in preference to being changed by someone he did not know.

It is especially important that staff should plan any outings to places of interest (see below) with the toileting needs of disabled children in mind, including, for example, taking adequate supplies of pads and locating the toilets to be used, in advance. (An account of the problems that can arise for children and staff, when this does not happen, is provided in Petrie *et al.*, 2000: 86–7.)

Outings

All the services in the study undertook visits off site even if these were only walks to the local park. Other outings included picnics, visits to the library as well as more ambitious outings to theme parks and tourist attractions. Earlier research (Petrie *et al.*, 2000: 86–8) suggested that any outings to places of interest should be thoroughly planned to take into account crossing roads, the location of toilets and changing facilities for disabled people, and the need to take on extra staff and volunteers in case of emergency. Services generally reported engaging additional staff for visits off site, to provide one-to-one support for children who in the more familiar indoor setting required no additional help. One playscheme had purchased a camping-style bedroll to take out so that they could ensure that a child who frequently had epileptic seizures could be made comfortable.

Our earlier research suggested that benefits to be derived from an outing need to be carefully weighed against the travelling time involved. Staff should, in advance of need, decide on their reaction to any discriminatory behaviour displayed by the public towards disabled children, and this should take into account both the needs of the child who has been insulted, as well as how to reply to the person who has been discriminatory or abusive.

6 Conclusions

There is no doubt that inclusive play services can be valuable resources for children, parents and the wider society. This study has indicated something of the range of local authority and voluntary agency practices in promoting inclusive services and the difficulties sometimes encountered. The study confirmed earlier findings that out-of-school services can indeed provide valuable play opportunities and friendships for disabled children, respite care for families who are hard pressed, and, in some cases, day care for working parents.

For social service departments, inclusive play services can be a useful addition to their repertoire of resources for families in need, taking the place in some cases of respite care services that are more expensive and less inclusive. Not least, they are means of reducing social isolation for parents and children, of introducing disabled and non-disabled children to each other and, potentially, of building a more inclusive society. As the number of mainstream out-of-school services increases, securing places for disabled children within them should be a matter of local authority play policy mirroring the objectives of the Quality Protects programme.

In some cases, the local infrastructure for mainstream play and youth services is as yet inadequate for the proper development of inclusive play facilities. Nevertheless, there is a growing understanding of good practice among some local authorities and voluntary organisations, upon which further developments can be built.

A useful starting point for the development of inclusive mainstream services are the Early Years and Care Development Partnerships, and this is already recognised in government guidelines. Regrettably, the study found that not all EYCDPs have been proactive in the development of inclusive play services. Yet they are ideally situated to be so, representing as they do a range of voluntary and local government agencies.

The following challenges need to be addressed:

- *Extending the number of out-of-school services prepared to take disabled children and finding ways of funding them so that they can attend at the same level as other children should be of priority.* Disabled children's attendance in play provision is usually rationed because providers have difficulty in obtaining funding for any extra staff required. This and other research suggest that there is much higher demand for places than is currently being met. As things are, inclusive services are rarely a reasonable basis for day care for working parents. Parents, for their part, mostly cannot afford to pay fees that would cover costs.

- *Training for inclusive practice should also be a component in all mainstream play and early years courses. This may be something for the newly formed Learning and Skills Councils to address.* The training and support of staff and volunteers is essential for the development of services in which staff feel confident, and parents secure, and where children interact positively, regardless of disability status. Goodwill is not sufficient to bring about a trained workforce: staff time and trainers' time all require funding – an essential prerequisite for inclusive services.

- *Not relying exclusively on key worker systems.* While inclusive play services need adequate staffing, this does not imply that every disabled child should be constantly attended by a key worker. This is a practice that can itself work against integration.

- *Consideration should be given to developing services for young people of secondary school age who may be placed, inappropriately, in settings used mainly by younger children.* While there has been some development in provision of play and care services for younger disabled children, youth services lag behind.

- *Local authority play, leisure and youth services should take responsibility for information reaching parents and children, for example through special schools, the Connexion service and special educational needs co-ordinators.* The parents of disabled school-age children can have difficulty in finding out about services.

- *Providers should be encouraged, whether at annual inspection or through funding mechanisms, to monitor ethnic intake in the context of the local population, to consider how ethnically representative their staff may be, and to review and/or develop their anti-racist policy* Minority ethnic groups may often be under-represented in out-of-school services. Truly inclusive services take children irrespective of disability status or ethnicity. (This area is developed more fully in Petrie *et al.*, 2000: sections 2 and 3.)

- *The development and support of such agencies is to be recommended at local and national level.* Both the local authority and voluntary development organisations can be effective in arranging and supporting placements for disabled children, changing the attitudes of providers, supplying training and developing good practice. However, voluntary agencies need financial support in order to be successful advocates for inclusive play.

Measures such as these are the necessary underpinning of the Quality Protects programme as it sets out to meet the needs of disabled children, and of meeting the requirements of the Disability Discrimination Act 1995.

As some of our informants reminded us, inclusivity is about fostering a mindset towards provision, about claiming social, physical and psychological accessibility for *all* children, on an equal footing, about fostering inclusive thinking among providers, staff, children, parents and, not least, local government departments. Inclusive services are for the benefit of the whole community, in part a frank acknowledgement that some of us have impairments. To deny impairment, by failing to make inclusive provision, can only impoverish the whole community through the exclusion of some of its members.

Appendices

APPENDIX 1: Study design and methods

Seventeen inclusive services were studied in six English local authorities, whose interagency action on behalf of disabled children was also researched. This work will be reported in a separate study, *Disabled Children at the Interface* (Petrie *et al.*, forthcoming). The sample included two rural authorities, two London authorities, authorities with larger and smaller ethnic minority populations, and authorities with different levels of children registered at risk. These authorities (the six joint-study authorities) were also chosen because they were reported to provide examples of good practice regarding inclusive play.

In addition, 15 services in eight further authorities were studied, in order to extend the range of possible models available for providing and supporting inclusive services.

The study was conducted mainly during the summer of 2000 and explored the following:

- local authority policy and practice regarding inclusive out-of-school services;
- the part played by local authority personnel in supporting and developing services and communicating with users about them;
- the part played by the voluntary sector in service development;
- funding and other support for inclusive services provision;
- service providers' policy and practice towards inclusive play.

These issues were explored via semi-structured interviews with senior personnel in different local authority departments (11 interviews with staff with responsibility for play services), senior staff in out-of-school services (32 interviews) and local voluntary-sector development workers (six interviews). Senior social service staff were interviewed in all six of the joint study authorities (but not in the remaining eight authorities).

Conversational interviews with disabled and non-disabled children explored their appreciation of inclusive play services in eleven of the services visited. This aspect of the study was affected by some children's understandable preference for play rather than talking with outsiders, by the constraints of the service timetable (e.g. outings to places of interest), short opening hours (e.g. after school services) and by communication difficulties between children and researchers, given the limited time available to get to know one another. (It should be noted that an earlier in-depth study of six services sought to obtain the children's own appreciation of services (Petrie *et al.*, 2000) and had sufficient time to overcome communication difficulties in a variety of ways.)

Local organisations facilitated the setting up of two focus groups to explore parents' experience of using out-of-school services. This was fewer than originally intended. The problem arose because of difficulties in timing meetings around the summer holiday period, when the research took place: there are often additional childcare duties for parents during school holidays, and some families take a holiday away from home.

APPENDIX 2: Useful organisations

Children's Play Council
8 Wakley Street
London
EC1V 7QE
Tel: 020 7843 6016
E-mail: cpc@ncb.org.uk
Website: www.ncb.org.uk/cpc/

Inclusive Play Opportunities Project
Salisbury Road
Barnet
Hertfordshire
EN5 4JP
Tel: 020 8441 0404
E-mail: ipop_ho@hotmail.com

Kidsactive
Pryor's Bank
London
SW6 3LA
Tel: 020 7731 1435
E-mail: pip@kidsactive.org.uk
Website: www.kidsactive.org.uk

Kids Clubs Network
Bellerive House
3 Muirfield Crescent
London
E14 9SZ
Tel: 020 7512 2112
E-mail: information.office@kidsclubs.org.uk
Website: www.kidsclubs.org.uk

London Play
Units F6–F7
89–93 Fonthill Road
London
N4 3JH
Tel: 020 7272 2464
E-mail: enquiries@londonplay.org.uk
Website: www.londonplay.org.uk

Markfield Project
Markfield Road
London
N15 4RB
Tel: 020 8800 4134

Mencap
123 Golden Lane
London
EC1Y 0RT
Tel: 020 7454 0454
E-mail: information@mencap.org.uk
Website: www.mencap.org.uk

The Parasol Project
Tower Play Base
Maltfield Road
Northway
Oxford
OX3 9RG
Tel: 01865 742 816
E-mail: parasol@oxford.communigate.co.uk
Website:
www.communigate.co.uk/oxford/parasol

Playboard Northern Ireland
59–65 York Street
Belfast
BT15 1AA
Tel: 028 9080 3380
E-mail: information@playboard.co.uk
Website: www.playboard.org/playboard

Playplus
11 Cornton Business Park
Cornton Road
Stirling
FK9 5AT
Tel: 01786 450 086

Play Wales
Baltic House
Mount Stuart Square
Cardiff Bay
Cardiff
CF10 5FH
Tel: 029 2048 6050
E-mail: mail@playwales.org.uk
Website: www.chwaraecymru.org.uk

Scottish Out-of-School Care Network
Fleming House
134 Renfrew Street
Glasgow
G3 6ST
Tel: 0141 331 1301
E-mail: info@soscn.org
Website: www.soscn.org

References

Audit Commission (1999) *Getting the Best from Children's Services: Findings from joint reviews of social services, 1998/99*. London: Audit Commission.

Beresford, B. (1995) *Expert Opinions: A national survey of parents caring for a severely disabled child*. Bristol: Policy Press.

DfEE (Department for Education and Employment) (2001) *EYDCPs: Planning guidance 2001–2002*. London: DfEE.

Department of Health (DoH) (1991) *Guidance and Regulations to the Children Act 1989: vol. 2*. London: HMSO.

Petrie, P. (1994) *Play and Care, Out-of-School*. London HMSO.

Petrie, P. and Poland, G. (1996) *After School and in the Holidays: A survey of provision*. London: Thomas Coram Research Unit, Institute of Education, University of London.

Petrie, P. and Poland, G. (1998) 'Play services for disabled children'. *Children and Society* 12: 283–94.

Petrie, P., Egharevba, I., Oliver, C. and Poland, G. (2000) *Out-of-school Lives, Out-of-School Services*. London: Stationery Office.

Petrie, P., Storey, P., Thompson, D. and Candappa, M. (forthcoming) *Children with Disabilities at the Interface: Co-operative action between public authorities and the reduction of social exclusion*. London: Institute of Education, University of London.

Thomas, M., Goddard, E., Hickman, M. and Hunter. P. (1994) *1992 General Household Survey*. London: HMSO.